Journey Down the Muddy Road

Calondra Grigsby

BookLeaf Publishing

Presentation by *BookLeaf Publishing*

Web: www.bookleafpub.com

E-mail: info@bookleafpub.com

ISBN: 9789357612883

First edition 2022

DEDICATION

This book is dedicated to Me, CG.

ACKNOWLEDGEMENT

I would like to thank Life, for just being who you are. It is unique to everyone and a lesson for some.
I want to thank my family, thank you for being supportive and understanding. Thank you for pushing me when I felt like giving up. Thank you for hugging me during the hard days.

Parents: I love you both and I know it's hard reading this but I'm sorry I was silent. I know you guys would have kicked tail, if I would have told you. I'm sorry I didn't give you the opportunity to do your part. Please forgive me.

PREFACE

98% of this book is true. Poetry and rhyming is not that easy when you are trying to get a point across. These poems reflect on the importance of protecting your children from everyone.
Speak to your children on a daily, making anything discussed a safe place. Be honest with your children and prepare them for the future.
These poems speak on how a traumatized childhood creates so many doors for the enemy to work with and failure.
Some poems speak on the healing process. Some poems are supposed to create laughter like Travel Sports and Women Issues.
My first book isn't perfect but it's good enough for me.

Muddy Road

Tired of Struggling,
And Living in the Past.

Living Lies, Living Fake,
At this rate I will age fast.

Tired of Looking Fresh
and on the Inside a mess.

Messy Life,
Messy Love,
A mess within a mess.

Tired of Hating myself
for the life that I lived.

Life of Lust,
Life of Addiction,
A life that seemed unreal.

Ready to forgive myself
and move on and believe.

Must walk the Muddy Road.
Shredding negativity from my past.

It will reveal my filth and my wrongs.
I can no longer sweep them under the rug.

Must walk the muddy road
At the end, I'll be cleaned.

Walk into a happy life,
Into self-love.
Walking in my destiny.

Poems 21MG QD

I just want to HEAL
Be set FREE
Writing all these poems please RELEASE the shame

Religion made me angry
Counseling points the blame
Writing these poems MUST HEAL ME

Each poem I write
Brings life to another past life ordeal
Healing is proof that ADDRESSSING mental health is real

I just want to be set free from what has been done to me
And I really need these poems to EXPRESS my apologies

Even if it sounds violent, gory, or sad
If these poems do not work
I am calling the Tuesday Night Goon Squad

Each poem that I write, to let go of this stronghold.

I have been holding this hurt and sorrow for
WAY TOO LONG

Lost 31:10-31

Who can find a virtuous woman?
Where the heck is she?
At school in my prep school uniform
and living in sin.
At grandma's I get raped
in the streets a feen.

Who can find a virtuous woman?
Man, can you find her for me?

Incest lowered my value and worth to about a buck.
Where every good guy I tried to pursue
Ended up getting hurt.
My clothes became more slutty
Because my body was my only worth

Who can find a virtuous woman.
It is not me and that really hurts.

The pennies that I received from laying on my back.
Landed me in poverty and a virtuous woman is not that.

Who can find a virtuous woman.
Wish I could find her within me

Who can find a virtuous woman
She is lost internally.

Stolen Property

Did you steal from me?
Something that was mine?
I could not even wash my ASS right.
Or even tell time

The images still haunt me,
to think you are Blood.

I cannot believe you used a child
to fulfill your lustful thoughts.

I can think of 50 different things
that you could have done,

But yo nasty tail decided
to use an innocent little child

You kept going happily
Even when I screamed OW!

I was used like a toy,
Little Rag doll.

You threw me 50 cents.
And I could not say a word,

I had to be the one
Or my little brother would have been the next
choice.

You stole my innocence and my childhood
I will never get that back

Or just to swing on a swing
And not be sore.

From that day on,
my life was never the same.

Years after you,
Passed down losing my soul.

I was just a little girl
silent and sexually abused.

I can never get it back
Because of your lustful nasty thoughts.

Give it back,
Give it back,
I just want it all back.

Mommy

A mother has flaws
But she is a protector, your first friend

Long talks on the phone
Advice to help you excel

She puts her life worries to the side
And will come to your beckoning aid

If you show up in her dreams,
she will wake up and begin to pray.

She prays over your life
and your everyday moves.

A mother makes sure you know
she will always love you.

She may be doing it alone,
so put your expectations aside.

A mother will fight for you
And always be your ride or die.

She is your nurse, your lawyer,
your tutor, and your chef.

Make sure to tell your mom,
thank you
You are the best.

No Role Model

Slowly disappearing from your life
I care about your heart.

You called me your role model
It made me re-evaluate my life

I had seen more for you
and would only get in your way

I was not the type of person
I thought you should follow and portray.

You may have seen something in me
that I did not see in myself.

The way I was living
would not have been good for your health.

I slowly disappeared
out of your life.

Me, being absent really worked
Look at you now,

you turned into a beautiful wife

from afar I am immensely proud

I slowly disappeared
So, you can grow and hold your crown

God Mom, Best Friend

Friendships are hard
so is communication

I was battling some demons
took decades to defeat them.

I missed many memories,
because of my past decisions

I hurt you and seen you cry,
and we have not spoken since.

I am glad that your flourishing
you really deserve the best.

One day I hope I get to apologize,
face to face, and make amends

Your God son is so Big
And you had a part in it.

Hoping my son will be able to meet his God
Mom
The one I called my best friend

“NO”

I said “No,” “Nah"," Nee,”
“Tidak” “Hayir” and “Ni”
I said no in some many ways,
and you still ignored me.

Whether I kicked, cried, screamed,
or said, ‘’I will call the Police.”
You did not care
You were going to rape me.

Your strength was too much,
and my fighting skills did not work.
Year after year,
the word “NO” is just not enough.

Tuesday Night Good Squad

Women young and women wise
Potluck type vibes
Come together and uplift each other
It is a Tuesday Night Vibe

From Worship and Movies
Armoring up to rebuke demons.
Providing Resources and Knowledge
A real shoulder to cry on

Getting together on Tuesday nights
Was better than hanging in the streets

You cannot beat a group of powerful women
That interceded and prayed over your kids.

That always have my back
Forever and always
Get together on Tuesday Night
and send me an Invite.

Warning Dreams

When we first met,
I had nightmares of my children being killed

I would take every bullet
so, they could escape and live

My oldest son would stand up
to protect his brothers and mom

You continued to shoot
not caring who you would harm.

Everyone seen so much in you
In life you were Charming and sweet

But the streets kept calling
And you could not resist.

I tried to love you
until you became a changed man.

If I would have stayed connected to you.
I would be mentally gone.

Qui Moi?

You Blame ME
The MOTHER of his kids
To set up a crime,
I would not wish on any head.

Yes, I pushed him to do his part
and help raise his kids

Never would I ever
Do such a Cruel EVIL thing

My kids would lose me too,
did you think about that?

You know he was not a good man.
Would love me
then beat me bad

My kids could not mourn their father
because of your ill thinking ways.

Your threats and lies
make me hate you until this very day.

My kids share his DNA

and now are the castaways.

This shit truly hurts
to even think about it.

I know people are reckless, look past me, I am
not it.

My kids love and miss their family,
but I must protect my kids.

Everything you put us through
as their mother I would never forget.
I cannot believe you blame me
I am still confused over this shit.

Qui Moi? Qui Moi?
Sometimes Stop and Think

Happy Father's Day

Happy Father's Day plaques
decorated with Love, Stickers, and Glue
Sitting in the box
collecting dust and waiting for you

When you were alive
You had walked past it
leaving our son hurt

Now your gone to another life
buried lifeless in earth's dirt

It is hard to see him process
this day each with tears

These plaques are our memories
of joy and pain from the years

I hope these memories teach him
the importance of being a good man and father
These Father's Day plaques now serve a bigger
purpose

Happy Father's Day plaques
decorated with stickers and glue

will remain in this box
as a lesson from You

Hello Face

Psychiatrist do not understand
only want to medicate

Every time I close my eyes,
I see so many faces.

So many faces I see
faces big, faces small.

I can even spot them on curtains,
wooden doors, and walls.

These faces are a sign
Whether a blessing or a curse.

I wonder if they would talk to me
if I said Hello Good day.

These faces I see will continue to pursue
One day I hope one of them will say Hello, how
are you.

Transform

Each poem is my life.
Where some topics really hurt.
My life has not been easy if you see me, it does not show.
A smile can hide sorrow and pain,
Laughter with jokes.

I am working on healing and every day is brand new.

I am a witness that things can look better,
with time and self-love.

Please do not live a life
of hurt, regret, or abuse.

Re-train your mind and take your time.
Transform into a new improved you.

Chicks for F'in Life

Like the crew from *Set it Off*
Or BET's *Girlfriends*

Harmonizing to "Meeting in my Bedroom"
Until the Road Trip ends.

Creating choreography to every song
Calling me out if I did wrong.

A listening ear when I need calmed.
A shoulder to cry on.

Standing behind me when I become a wife.
A helping hand when facing strife.

I have the best ladies around
I call my Chicks For F'in Life

Prolapsed

Minding my business
chillen with my friends

Laughing and dancing
to the Ying Yang Twins

Something strange happened,
creating moisture between my leg.

Under 40 years old
and I could not hold my bladder
I had to go.

The doctor said it's normal
for a mother with 4 kids.

Kegel exercises and therapy
I was prescribed to complete.

It can happen if I laugh,
cry, or lay down.

It happens during car rides,
roller coaster and concerts now.

Potholes are the worse,
do not get me started on that.

I must bring extra clothes,
and a little travel bag.

Do not judge me when you see me
and I have a new outfit on.
It is not my fault, I blame the big-headed little
ones

Big Words

Big words, big words
keep them to yourself

They are just a waste a time
make you run out of breath.

They make you sound intelligent
but takes up too much time.

I will look up and down
if you make me process just too much.

Like:
Love is endearment
Hate abominate
Draw is Illustrate
And praise congratulate

One to two syllables
versus saying four to eight.

Simple is the key
to effectively communicate.

ADHD

Passwords change
Lost Keys
Finishing Assignments
Help Please!

Calendar confused
Laundry behind
only about
a month or two.

I will always answer yes
No just seems too hard to say

I thought of all of this while changing a password.
And this is a good day

Love Song

He turned my “Ready for Love” into “Steady Love”
Rocking the sheets like “Sweet Love”

making him the “Greatest Love”
Ooh, he got me “Drunk in Love”
Vibing to “Forever” and “Love”

He makes me “Weak” in the knees
“Don’t Change” Baby please.
He is my “Brotha” “My Rock”
Thank you for your “Respect” towards me

Hope we can “Make it last forever”
"He proposed” and I said, “I do”

“Grow Old with Me” “Always and Forever”
Baby "I believe in You and Me”

Organic Pleasure

Celibate for a Year
Seemed very impossible.
Dibbled and dabbled with toys.
But that was not working.

A trip to the grocery store.
These veggies got me flowing.
A cucumber and banana helped expand the imagination.
An Egg Plant was too much, why do they grow so big.
The Organic section makes my juices flow better than a ***.

J/K
Organic Pleasure

Travel Sports

Sign me up for stretch mark night at the
gentlemen's club.
I need to do something to pay $2400 bucks.

We do not need new uniforms
just a permanent marker and a court.

We can even Tie Dye T-shirt
and bring your own shorts.

Geez, Travel Ball Travel Ball, Rec Leagues Will
Do.
Travel Ball, Travel Ball, Rec League will do.

Baseball Bat and Gloves cost more than an
electric bill.
Traveling early morning,
and the gas prices are unreal.

Geez, Travel Ball Travel Ball, Rec Leagues Will
Do.
Travel Ball, Travel Ball, Rec League will do

Parents with no coffee are the funniest to see.
Cooler, lawn chairs, wagons, and games.

Travel Ball and Rec League they both are insane.
I will still sign my kids up; they better enter the Hall of Fame.

www.ingramcontent.com/pod-product-compliance
Lightning Source LLC
Chambersburg PA
CBHW062204160726
48282CB00027B/986
* 9 7 8 9 3 5 7 6 1 2 8 8 3 *